President, TERAGRAM Coaching & Consulting Group

"A simple and understandable approach to the organizing process. Hellen and Sari help you discover your unique learning style and the organizing approach that's right for you. If your previous attempts to get organized have proved futile, this book is for you."

– Barry Iszak, CPO®, CRTS, Past President of National Association of Professional Organizers, and author, Organize Your Garage in No Time

"*Organizing Outside the Box* is a great addition to the professional organizer's toolkit and a must read for those who have found that nothing seems to work."
– Harold Taylor, bestselling author, Making Time Work for You

"Hellen is a master at helping people declutter their lives and become happier and more successful. Buy this book and see how great you can be."
– Grace Cirocco, author, Take the Step, the Bridge Will Be There

"This small book delivers big with practical organizing methods that suit you best. It is fast-paced, compelling, and comprehensive."
– Bill Roebuck, Editor-in-Chief, Home Digest Magazine

"This simple, practical, and effective book guides readers through the chaos of clutter to take charge of their world."
– George Torok, co-author of Secrets of Power Marketing and radio host of Business in Motion

"*Organizing Outside the Box* gave me tools and techniques specific to my learning style, bringing more organization and energy into my daily life."
– Natasha Maciel, busy wife, mother of two, and Business Coach

Organizing Outside the Box

Conquer Clutter Using Your Natural Learning Style

HELLEN BUTTIGIEG
CPO®

SARI BRANDES
M.Ed.

BPS
books

Published in 2009 by BPS Books Toronto, Canada
www.bpsbooks.com
A division of Bastian Publishing Services Ltd.

ISBN 978-1-926645-09-4

Canadian Cataloguing in Publication Data available from Library and Archives Canada

Cover design: Gnibel
Text design and typesetting: Kinetics Design www.kdbooks.ca
Cover photo: Tim Leyes

Mind Map diagram created in Inspiration® (Kidspiration® or InspireData®) by Inspiration Software®, Inc. Pendaflex® and Pendaflex PileSmart® are registered trademarks of Esselte Corporation.

Publisher's Note
Any mention in this book of a brand name product or company should not be considered an endorsement. The names of any clients mentioned in this book are fictional.

Printed by Lightning Source, Tennessee. Lightning Source paper, as used in this book, does not come from endangered old growth forests or forests of exceptional conservation value. It is acid free, lignin free, and meets all ANSI standards for archival-quality paper. The print-on-demand process used to produce this book protects the environment by printing only the number of copies that are purchased.

*Dedicated to anyone who
has ever felt overwhelmed
by chaos in their lives.*

*May you be inspired by a
fresh approach to life balance
that celebrates who you are.*

Contents

Acknowledgments	9
Introduction	13
How to Use this Book	17
Quiz: Determine Your Learning Style	19

I Organizing That Fits Your Learning Style

1 Organizing as a Visual Learner: 27
Seeing Is Remembering

• Do You Fit the Profile of a Visual Learner?	27
• Case Study: Meet Marcia	28
• Ready, Set, Go	31
• Organizing Strategies for the Visual Learner	32
• Staying Organized	41

2 Organizing as a Kinesthetic Learner: 43
Doing Is Remembering

• Do You Fit the Profile of a Kinesthetic Learner?	44
• Case Study: Meet Susan	45
• Ready, Set, Go	47
• Organizing Strategies for the Kinesthetic Learner	48
• Staying Organized	56

3 Organizing as an Auditory Learner: 59
Hearing Is Remembering

• Do You Fit the Profile of an Auditory Learner?	59

- Case Study: Meet Michelle   61
- Ready, Set, Go   63
- Organizing Strategies for
     the Auditory Learner   63
- Staying Organized   70

4 When Organizing Styles Collide   73
- Organizing Strategies When Dealing
     with Different Learning Styles   73

II **Organizing at Home**

5 When Organizing Styles Collide at Home   79
- Ready, Set, Go   79
- How to Blend Styles   80
- Staying Organized   82

6 When Organizing Styles Collide with Children   85
- Ready, Set, Go   85
- How to Blend Styles   87
- Staying Organized   91

III **Organizing at Work**

7 When Organizing Styles Collide at Work   95
- Ready, Set, Go   95
- How to Blend Styles   96
- Staying Organized   98

Conclusion   99
Further Resources   103

Acknowledgments

From Hellen

A big thank-you to:

My husband, Victor. If it were not for your belief in me and your constant encouragement, this book would not exist.

My children, Sarah and Michelle. You have taught me that we are all unique in our own way and that this is a good thing.

My parents, Mike and Anastasia. You were my first teachers and excellent role models for living an organized life.

My first coach, my mentor, and my friend, Margaret Miller, for helping me find the courage to take the leap and start my business.

My agent, Lilana Novakovich, for putting me in front of the best audiences in the world.

My production crew on the show *neat*, for making it fun to go to work every day, despite the long hours.

HGTV Canada, for believing in the show and giving us three successful seasons.

All of the fans of the show, for letting me into your living room and making the show such a success.

Professional Organizers in Canada, for the lifelong friendships I've made with the most compassionate, yet efficient, people in the world.

City Centre Toastmasters in Mississauga, for taking a stay-at-home mom seriously when I said I wanted to be a speaker.

The members of the Toronto chapter of the Canadian Association of Professional Speakers, for generously sharing your expertise with me.

All of my clients, for bravely allowing me and my associates into your homes, in the process motivating us to find better solutions for your organizing challenges.

Last but not least, I wish to thank all my friends, who have had to put up with me talking about this book for years before I finally put pen to paper. I've always felt that success is nothing unless you have someone to share it with, and all of you were there for me.

From Sari

My warmest thanks to:

Pearl, for being my inspiration. You have shown me time and time again that with hard work and creativity a person can do anything.

Marshal and Lisa, for helping me to get started on this wild ride and always cheering me on. You were – and are – always there with support, creative problem solving, and advice.

Hyim and Dahnie, for teaching me patience, for helping me to build my business, and for all your love, assistance, and encouragement.

Bobby, for your advice and your special way of always being there when I need you.

The families that I work with, who are the inspiration for this work, who give me the opportunity to join you on your journeys of change, and who have helped me to build a career that fulfills me and gives me joy.

And special thanks to my parents, Susan and

Eytan, for making sure I had all the tools for success. You have always believed in me and never even blinked when I aimed for something that I thought was far beyond my reach. Instead, you were always optimistic and lent support and assistance. You have never wavered in your love and constant belief in my abilities. You are my role models, my mentors. All my thanks and love. I owe everything to you.

Introduction

When it comes to getting organized, have you ever felt like a square peg trying to fit into a round hole?

You've tried to get organized in the past. You've bought enough books on the topic to open your own library. You can't resist buying any magazine that has the words "clutter" or "organize" on the cover. And you've become addicted to watching the organizing shows on TV.

And yet there you are, still surrounded by piles of papers, crammed closets, and a garage full of everything but your car. All those great tips that work for everyone else just don't seem to work for you. You feel like a disorganized misfit.

However, think about when you try on a sweater that is too big or too small: The problem isn't you; the problem is the size of the sweater. The same is true when it comes to organizing. It's the solution, not you, that's the problem.

Organizing isn't one size fits all. There are many ways to organize your space, your time, and your life. In general, no one way is better or worse than another. No two people are alike: A useful organizing tip may not work as well for you as it does for someone else. It might even make matters worse.

The key to getting organized once and for all is to find a solution that fits your learning style.

This book contains techniques that are tailored for you according to your natural and preferred way of learning, communicating, and thinking. It is based on insights from the latest research into learning styles.

The central point of this book is that your optimal organizing style stems from your preferred learning style. There are three main styles: visual, auditory, and kinesthetic. We all have overlapping styles but usually favor one.

Discovering your natural and preferred learning style and using organizing techniques that reflect it will make it easier for you to get organized. And the results will last longer because they will come naturally.

Furthermore, a major bonus of this book is that it will help you to understand other people's learning and organizing styles so you can harmonize your style with those who live with or work with you.

Finally, getting organized in these spheres can enable you to live an organized life in a broader sense.

Once you discover your personal organizing style

and learn how to set up systems that work well for you and others, you will begin to live a more joyful and productive life.

And that's why getting organized is so important: It frees you from getting hung up on the non-essential so you can truly enjoy the essential.

How to
Use this Book

We encourage you to read this book in the way that feels right for you. However, here are some suggestions:

1 Take the quiz to determine your learning style.

2 Read the chapter that matches your learning style.

3 Take notes. Remember, this is your book, so use it to organize your thoughts in a way that makes it easy for you to retrieve and act on them later. You may want to annotate the pages, use sticky notes, use a highlighter, or take notes in a separate notebook – whatever comes most naturally to you.

4 Specifically, write ideas, inspirations, and action steps as they come to you. You may also want to record ideas for sharing with others.

5 Pick a method for keeping track of tasks/to-do's based on your learning style and use the method to keep track of your action steps. Action steps are a to-do list of concrete activities that will move you closer to your goals.

6 Try the suggested techniques that fit your style.

7 Then go back and read the chapters that deal with the other learning and organizing styles to see if some of the techniques described there may help you, given your particular combination of learning preferences.

8 Continue using the techniques you settle on for one month.

9 At the end of the month, go back and evaluate what works, what needs to be adjusted, and what may not be working for you.

10 Use the book's techniques to help others in your life learn to organize themselves. When you allocate tasks to them, do so in a way that speaks to *their* specific style.

Quiz:

Determine Your Learning Style

To take this quiz online, visit organizingoutsidethebox.com

1 I would rather read a
- **A** magazine
- **B** novel
- **C** Website

2 If I am reading a book, I prefer
- **A** one with a lot of pictures and charts
- **B** fiction
- **C** a graphic novel or comic

3 In a restaurant, what distracts me most is
- **A** loud music
- **B** too many decorations on the walls
- **C** drawing on the table

4 When I have to make a large decision, I
- **A** think about it in a quiet place
- **B** make lists
- **C** think about it while moving around

5 When I need to make a decision, I
- **A** talk to my friends and family
- **B** read about the subject
- **C** go with my gut

6 *When choosing clothes, I*
  - A like to wear my favorite things most of the time
  - B take my time and find the right match
  - C take what's clean or the first thing I see

7 *In meetings, I*
  - A listen and remember
  - B take lots of notes and try to get everything important on paper
  - C write only what pertains to me, frequently doodling the rest of the time

8 *When relating a story to a friend, I*
  - A start at the beginning and tell the entire story
  - B tell the main point and fill in details only when I have to
  - C jump around from one important idea to the next

9 *When I am anxious, I*
  - A talk over in my head what worries me most
  - B visualize the worst-case scenarios
  - C can't sit still, fidget, and move around constantly

10 *I speak with*
  - A few gestures
  - B no gestures
  - C many gestures

11 *I remember best what I*
  - A said and heard
  - B saw
  - C did

12 *I like to*
  A be read to
  B read silently
  C read aloud to others

13 *When trying new things, I*
  A look at the diagrams in the directions and then jump in, coming back to the directions only if I need them
  B read and follow the directions systematically
  C ignore the directions and use the trial-and-error method

14 *When I need help, I*
  A ask others
  B research
  C look around and see what others are doing

15 *In my free time, I like to*
  A listen to music or talk with friends
  B read or play on the computer
  C go out and do something

16 *When playing a game, I tend to*
  A pay close attention to the other players and what they are doing
  B watch the board or screen and plan my next moves
  C get very excited

17 *I most readily remember*
  A lyrics or words
  B tunes
  C what I was doing when I heard that song

18 I find it easier to remember

   A names

   B faces

   C where I met someone and what we were doing

19 I react to

   A the tone in which something is said

   B the literal meaning of what is said

   C the manner in which something is said (body language and volume)

20 In my free time, I like to

   A watch TV, listen to music, or talk to friends on the phone

   B read or surf the web

   C do something active

21 When I operate new equipment, I generally

   A listen to an explanation from someone who has used it before

   B read the instructions first

   C jump in and figure it out as I go

22 When I concentrate, I usually

   A think about the problem and the possible solutions in my head

   B close my eyes or stare into space

   C move around a lot, fiddle with pens and pencils, and touch things

23 I purchase things because I like

   A the descriptions the salespeople give me

   B their colors and how they look

   C their textures and what it feels like to touch them

Results

Now add up how many A's, B's, and C's you selected.

A's =_____   *B's* =_____   *C's* = _____

A If you chose mostly **A's**, you have an *auditory* learning style.

B If you chose mostly **B's**, you have a *visual* learning style.

C If you chose mostly **C's**, you have a *kinesthetic* learning style.

You may find that you have a combination of learning styles. Most people have dominance in one area but still come up strong in another. If this is the case for you, read the chapters for both learning styles, beginning with the one that covers your dominant style.

I

Organizing
That Fits Your

Learning
Style

1

Organizing as a
Visual Learner

Seeing Is Remembering

You know you're a visual learner if you pile clothing, paperwork, and other items on the floor, table, or any other flat surface you can find, yet your closets, drawers, and filing cabinets are almost empty.

You like to keep things out where you can see them because, for you, out of sight is out of mind.

Yet with so much to look at, you can become easily distracted and lose focus.

Do You Fit the Profile of a Visual Learner?

You fit if you:

- Like to keep things out where you can see them
- Find colors appealing
- Are easily distracted in noisy environments
- Need to see things to remember (out of sight = out of mind)

- Like to write things down
- Follow written directions best
- Learn best by observing
- Close your eyes or look up or down while thinking
- Learn best with visual aids (pictures, diagrams, and videos)
- Have an artistic side
- Remember faces but not names

Your interests may include:

- Reading
- Watching movies
- Drawing

Career interests for visual learners may include:

- Sculptor
- Visual artist
- Inventor
- Architect
- Interior designer
- Mechanic
- Engineer
- Surgeon
- Teacher
- Writer

Case Study: Meet Marcia

Is this your story, too?

Marcia is a people person in her mid-thirties who works in the film industry.

When I first met Marcia, she told me she was doing relatively well in her career but felt she could be doing better.

Marcia did a lot of work from home because she found the noise in her shared office distracting.

However, she was frustrated in her home office, too – by the amount of time she was wasting looking for missing papers. She confided that she sometimes watched TV instead of working on her projects because she was overwhelmed by the mess on her desk.

She sometimes put tasks off until the last minute and then had to work late into the night to meet deadlines.

"I'm happiest when I have a lot of irons in the fire," she said. "But I often have trouble deciding which project to work on at any given time."

Although she is excited at the beginning of a new project, she often loses interest along the way and abandons it.

When I asked her why she wanted to get organized, she closed her eyes and thought about her answer for a few seconds.

"Because I'm feeling bogged down by all the piles of papers all over my apartment," she said. "And I'm tired of wasting time looking for things."

Marcia added that she knew she could put that time to better use to further her career. She mentioned that lack of sleep caused by stress was taking a toll on her mood and her health.

Assessing the space

When I took a closer look at her workspace and the rest of her apartment, the first thing I noticed were the colorful sticky notes she had attached to her computer, her phone, her mirror, and even the inside of her front door.

And her refrigerator was covered with magnets that held up scraps of paper with notes scribbled on them and a few photos.

Her bulletin board was overflowing – parts of it were actually five layers thick.

I found that the drawers of her filing cabinet were empty except for a few thin files – files that she had long forgotten about.

I asked her about the several bags of new clothing sitting beside her front door.

"They're the wrong fit or wrong color," she said. "I keep them there as a reminder to return them to the store."

As for her bedroom, clean clothes were strewn on the floor, piled on chairs, and overflowing from the laundry basket.

Her drawers and closet were underutilized. Dirty clothes were piled on top of the laundry hamper rather than placed inside it.

Finding the fit

Although I had quickly spotted many clues to Marcia's learning style in her surroundings, I asked her a few more questions to confirm my assessment.

I asked her what she was like in a learning environment. She described herself as liking to sit in the front where she had a clear view of the speaker.

"I always take detailed notes, though I don't always refer back to them," she said.

Marcia told me that in fitness classes, she can follow and learn the routine when the instructor actually demonstrates the moves but not when the instructor talks the class through them.

Asked what she was like when learning a new skill, Marcia responded that she always read the directions and looked at the diagrams when assembling new furniture or figuring out how to use a new product.

I determined that Marcia was a visual learner.

Ready, Set, Go

Motivating the visual learner to get started

Beginning the decluttering process is usually the hardest part. Putting it off makes the task seem all the more daunting.

Here are some tips on how to get the ball rolling if you're a visual learner.

- Find pictures in magazines of what you want your space to look like.
- Block off regular times in your calendar to work on decluttering a little at a time.
- Do one space or room at a time. You will feel less overwhelmed, and success with each space will motivate you to move on to the next.
- Use colored bags or place different-colored sheets in front of boxes for sorting. Choose four colors that make sense to you and label them:
  - Keep

- Give away
- Toss
- Move elsewhere

Organizing Strategies for the Visual Learner

Organizing preference

You like to keep everything out where you can see it.

Organizing problems

You can't find what you need and feel overwhelmed with everything scattered around the room.

If you're a visual learner, you will likely want to keep everything out where you can see it. You may be afraid to put things in drawers or closets because you might forget where you put them. In the past, you may have stored things out of sight only to purchase duplicates because you couldn't find the originals when you needed them or forgot you had them in the first place.

But keeping items out in the open can create a visual overload for you. Visual people can become overstimulated when they have too much to look at.

This certainly was the case with Marcia. She felt both overwhelmed and distracted by the piles of stuff around her. It was clogging her creativity and dimming her focus. She was missing deadlines and feeling frustrated.

Can you relate to Marcia? Are the piles in your house or apartment growing so high that it's becoming difficult to see what's at the bottom? Are you wasting time looking for important documents?

How can you satisfy your natural preference to keep things out yet still be able to find what you need?

Organizing solutions

Following are some tools and techniques you can use that fit your "everything out" preference.

Remove the obstacles

Anything that blocks your view is preventing you from using the space optimally.

- Choose shelving and other open storage systems and use them instead of dresser drawers for clothing. Place smaller items in baskets on low shelves so you can still see what's inside.
- Remove sliding doors from closets and replace with drapes that easily glide out to the sides or with doors that swing outward.
- Closets are not just for hanging items on hangers. Install stackable shelving units or use hanging sweater organizers inside your closets. Place folded t-shirts, tank tops, or handbags inside the compartments. You can also slide baskets inside the cubbies to store small, loose items like socks, undergarments, and scarves.

Stackable shelving unit

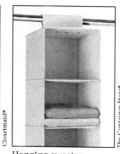

Hanging sweater organizer

Eliminate visual distractions

- Turn the TV off when you want to focus on your work.
- Make sure you have plenty of good lighting. Avoid fluorescent lights. Full-spectrum lights reduce fatigue and will help you to maintain your concentration.
- If you have your desk in front of a window, reposition it so you're not distracted by what's going on outside. An alternative is to close the blinds or drapes.
- If you are seated facing the doorway, reposition your desk so you are sideways to the door instead. This will prevent hallway activity from interfering with your concentration. It's best not to have your back to the doorway, because you may be startled when people walk in. Another option is to close the door when you need to focus.
- Sit facing away from photos, artwork, or a crammed bulletin board. Having these visual distractions directly in your line of sight can be overstimulating, causing you to tire before you've completed your work.
- If you can't reconfigure your office to eliminate external distractions, consider working in another room (e.g., the boardroom) when you're on a deadline and have to stay on task.

Make clear plastic bins your best friend
Clear containers allow you to easily see what you've stored inside.

- Before shopping for containers, measure the

spaces where they'll be placed and jot down the dimensions of what you need. You may find it helpful to take along some photos of the things you plan to store in the containers.

- Store similar items together and label the contents.
- If dust is not an issue, you can eliminate lids for easier access to your items.
- Keep the bins on adjustable shelves.
- Avoid stacking any bins you need to access regularly.
- Place the bins you use most often within arm's reach. Store the ones you use only occasionally below them. Bins that are used rarely should be stored on higher shelves. If the contents of the containers are heavy, avoid storing them on high shelves, for safety reasons. Store them on the lower shelves instead.

Get hooked on hooks

When it comes to hooks, there are countless options on the market. You can use over-the-door hooks, adhesive hooks, and hooks that screw into the wall. Use a variety for different purposes, but use them as much as you can.

- Place the outfit you plan to wear the next day on a coat tree.
- Place your robe on an over-the-door hook.
- Display your jewelry on cup hooks screwed into the wall in the closet.

Over-the-door hooks

- Keep a clear bag on a hook for dry-cleaning or hand-wash items.
- Hang your pots and pans and tools and craft supplies on pegboard-and-hook systems.
- Over-the-door pocket organizers designed for shoes can be used to store office supplies, toiletries, small toys, or wardrobe accessories. The clear pockets allow you to see what you've stored inside. Hanging an item takes up very little space.

The Container Store®

Over-the-door
pocket organizer

Use open filing systems

You can take the fear out of filing by using open filing systems. Because let's face it: If you've never used your filing cabinets fully, you probably never will. Get rid of them.

- Store your files in crates or rolling carts. These are open at the top, giving you a clear view and easy access.
- Keep your filing system within arm's reach of your desk to encourage you to file as you go.

Office Depot®

Rolling file cart

- Scan as much as possible. Use scanning software that will allow you to find documents by searching for the key words you entered. This will give you fast and easy access to documents without having

to keep the originals. This will serve to decrease
the amount of filing you have to do.

- Files that you use daily (hot files) can be stored
  in a step-sorter, a literature sorter, or a file box
  on your desktop or credenza.
  - A step-sorter, or incline sorter, is a tiered stand
    that you can slip your files into. Each folder
    will sit slightly higher
    than the one in front
    of it, making it easy
    for you to view and
    retrieve files. Choose
    clear plastic or mesh
    whenever possible and
    go for the larger size
    so you can store
    many folders.

Step-sorter

  - A literature sorter
    usually has three
    vertical and at least
    eight horizontal
    compartments to

Literature sorter

    store your documents and may be constructed
    of economical, lightweight corrugated paper,
    melamine laminated
    wood, fiberboard, or
    high-impact plastic.
  - A desktop file box is
    open at the top and
    sometimes includes
    hanging file folders
    and tabs. It may be

Desktop file box

made of plastic, mesh, or wicker. It comes in both letter and legal sizes.

○ Clear plastic letter trays are effective for an inbox, outbox, and for papers waiting to be filed. Avoid stacking them because you may forget about the bottom trays.

Filers vs. pilers

If you're a piler, you may prefer to use a literature sorter (see page 37) or letter trays to organize your paperwork. You may also want to try

Desktop organizer tray

putting the desktop organizer tray on your desk to keep that pile manageable and papers easy to retrieve. This is a fit with your natural habit of stacking papers flat.

If you're a filer, you may prefer a vertical filing system like a rolling cart (see page 36), crate, or desktop file box (see page 37).

Either way, use open top filing systems to eliminate your fear that out of sight = out of mind.

Color your world

Visual learners remember by seeing. Associating different colors for different types of information or tasks will help you to find things quickly.

Don't go overboard with color-coding, though: It's difficult to remember color associations when you go beyond nine colors.

Keep your code consistent; use the same colors for the same things at work and at home.

Choose colors according to your personal associations: for example, green for financial, blue for business, and red for action.

- Sort objects using different-colored bags. For example, use black for trash, orange for giveaway items, and clear for move elsewhere.
- Create color-filing systems using one standard color to identify all similar project files.
- Use different-colored loose-leaf binders to distinguish between different projects. Put colored plastic folders or tabs inside.
- For larger projects, use accordion files or pocket folders in various colors.
- Use color settings on your computer calendar to differentiate between work and social commitments.
- Assign each family member a different color to track their activities on the family calendar.
- Designate different-colored bins for each family member's accessories (hats, gloves) and store on a shelf in the mudroom or hallway closet.
- Use notebooks with colored sections and dividers for your lists of projects, things to buy, movies to watch, books to read, etc.
- Use sticky notes in various colors inside your planner to highlight important events or actions to take.
- Use bright highlighters to make key information stand out in books, magazines, and reports that you will refer to again.

- Use clear or see-through files for current/ in-progress and action files.
- Use colored paper clips as action reminders. For example:
  - Red = action needed immediately
  - Blue = progress
  - Green = take the file to the meeting
  - Yellow = to be filed
- Look for colored clips with space for labeling.

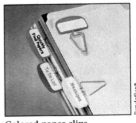

Colored paper clips

Pendaflex®

Use notebooks and calendars

Writing things down helps you to remember things by placing them into long-term memory. And what you record works as a backup system for when you are overloaded with thoughts, ideas, and projects on the go.

Following are some ways to keep your important reminders safe and organized.

- Small notebooks are great to keep in your pocket or purse for writing down shopping lists and to-do lists as items occur to you. Be sure to keep one handy at all times so you can review it and add to it consistently.
- If you are a note taker, use notebooks with sections. Keep like types of notes together in sections. These sections could include:
  - Departmental notes
  - Your ideas and inspirations
  - Notes for various projects
  - Call logs

- If you use paper calendars, find ones that have space for notes and to-do lists. Keeping all of your information in one place makes it more likely that you will remember to check your appointments and tasks more often.

- Technology can be a great tool. Learn to use the reminder settings on your cellphone, PDA, or computer. Set reminders not just for appointments but also for important to-do items.

- Do a search for applications for your phone or PDA; many have programs for little or no cost that will sync them and your computer so phone numbers you insert onto either will appear on the other. Some phones and PDAs also allow you to add your numbers to a family member's list, and vice versa. There is also a program that uses GPS to set off an alarm if you are in the vicinity of one of the locations with a to-do task. For example, if you are near your market, it will remind you of your shopping list or tell you that you have dry cleaning to pick up.

Staying Organized

Maintenance strategies for the visual learner

- Write any actions you must take on a to-do list in your notebook and schedule time on your calendar for taking action.

- Schedule time daily to go over your actions and appointments for that day (this can also be done the night before).

- Schedule a day and time in your calendar that you will consistently use to plan the upcoming week.

- Schedule time to do your filing each week.
- Resist bringing papers into your home or office unless you have a specific plan for how you'll use them. Whenever possible, file only the necessary information: Keep a note of the source rather than all the paperwork itself, in case you need to look the material up some day. Sources can include Websites, names and phone numbers, and names of books or magazines.
- List your current projects on individual cards and put them on a bulletin board. Limit the amount of projects on the go at any one time to a number that is manageable for you. Use the one-in-one-out rule: Start a new project only once a current one has been completed.
- Clear your desk or work surface before starting new projects. Put away the supplies and paperwork for one project before beginning the next one.
- Introduce just one or two new systems a month to avoid overload. Use your new systems consistently and modify them as you go along to best fit your needs. Resist giving up entirely on a system. Usually all it needs is some tweaking to fit you better (similar to how a new suit in your size may still need a few alterations).
- Reassess systems after any major life change, such as career, marriage, divorce, childbirth, and so on. Although your style will remain consistent, your needs will not remain the same forever. Schedule time to re-evaluate and modify your systems when necessary.

2

Organizing as a
Kinesthetic Learner

Doing Is Remembering

You know you're a kinesthetic learner if you need to be in constant motion.

Whether you're reading, talking, or listening, you cannot sit still for long. You have a tendency to talk with your hands and frequently use the sense of touch.

You like to have music on in the background when you're working on tasks and tend to take frequent breaks, often to get snacks. You learn best by watching and doing.

Because you are action oriented, you tend to start doing things without waiting for instructions. You prefer the trial-and-error method over taking things step by step.

You like to be involved in several activities at once. You are quickly bored and easily distracted. Yet with so much on the go, you're always in a rush and often don't have the time to put away supplies from one activity before moving on to the next.

Do You Fit the Profile of a Kinesthetic Learner?

You fit if you:

- Learn best through hands-on activities
- Tend to wiggle while you work
- Like to take risks and experiment
- Have a good sense of direction
- Need to take frequent breaks
- Like to get up and move around
- Skip directions and just do it
- Become bored or distracted if you don't have regular changes of pace
- Like to tip your chair
- Are spontaneous
- Do your best thinking moving around, exercising, or lying down

Your interests may include:

- Dancing
- Acting
- Cooking
- Sports and other physical activities

Career interests for kinesthetic learners include:

- Athlete
- Fitness instructor/gym teacher
- Dancer
- Actor
- Firefighter
- Sculptor
- Construction worker

- Mechanic
- Adventure tour leader
- Personal trainer
- Clothing designer
- Chemist
- Speaker/trainer/facilitator
- Human resources consultant

Case Study: Meet Susan

Is this your story, too?

Susan is a student in her early twenties who is working several part-time jobs as a dance instructor while studying to be a play therapist. She is also a member of a running club and works out at the gym almost every day.

When I met Susan, she told me she was doing well juggling all her activities but felt stressed about her disorganized apartment.

"I keep every piece of paper and book in case I might need it later, even if I've completed the course," she told me.

As a result, she said, she was often frustrated because she couldn't quickly put her hands on the notes she needed.

Susan did exceptionally well during the fieldwork portion of her program but had difficulty sitting down long enough to study and get her homework done.

"Whenever I sit down to work, I lose interest," she said. "I get up to have a snack or surf the net. Then I lose track of time and have to rush or stay up late to finish my assignments."

Susan told me she is happiest when creating dance routines for her students or engaging in play therapy with the children during her fieldwork assignments.

When I asked her why she wanted to get organized, she started to fidget with her pen and then admitted that she would feel so much better if she wasn't always racing against the clock.

"If I could just get my homework over with quickly, I would feel less anxious and spend more time having fun."

Assessing the space

When I took a closer look at her space, the first thing I noticed was the exercise equipment in various corners of her apartment. She had an exercise ball, elastic exercise bands, even a large mat.

I noted that her desk was covered in paper and her pens were all mangled and chewed.

She had disassembled her toaster with the intention of fixing it but hadn't got around to it.

Her cat had every toy imaginable strewn about the apartment. Susan told me proudly that she spends lots of time playing with him.

I noticed a variety of textures in her space: satin pillows, fuzzy blankets, and chiffon drapes.

There were lots of clothes, shoes, and handbags in her closet.

"I confess – I'm a shopaholic," she said with a rueful smile. "I'm always getting bored with my wardrobe."

Susan admitted to being a pack rat.

"You never know when you're going to need something," she said.

Her kitchen countertops bristled with lots of gadgets, including an ice-crusher, a sandwich maker, and an electric can opener.

Finding the fit

Although I had quickly spotted many clues to Susan's learning style in her surroundings, I asked her a few more questions to confirm my assessment.

I asked her what she was like in a learning environment.

"When I attend classes, I like to sit at the end of a row," she said. "That way I can move my legs and get out quickly if I need a drink or to go to the bathroom."

She added that she could easily remember information when the teacher demonstrated it. She often volunteered to get involved in the demonstration, especially when it included role playing.

Asked what she was like when learning a new skill, she said, "I get bored reading or listening to instructions. I prefer to just go ahead and figure it out along the way."

I determined that Susan was a kinesthetic learner.

Ready, Set, Go

Motivating the kinesthetic learner to get started

Beginning the decluttering process is usually the hardest part. Putting it off makes the task seem all the more daunting.

Here are some tips on how to get the ball rolling if you're a kinesthetic learner:

- Set a timer and play beat-the-clock to make it fun and prevent boredom.
- Give yourself permission to take regular breaks but set a time limit on them. Anything longer than thirty minutes and you may not get back to what you were doing.
- Write your to-do list on a large whiteboard (or other large writing surface) and draw a big box beside each item. Position the whiteboard on your wall so you have to get up and walk over to it to check items off as you complete them.
- Prepare healthful snacks ahead of time in one-serving portions and keep them handy.
- When wading through your papers or tackling your closet, put some music on and spread out your sorting bins so you can travel several steps between them.
- Assign different corners of the room to different categories.
- Place things on a table and stand up to organize them rather than organizing while sitting down.

Organizing Strategies for the Kinesthetic Learner

Organizing preference
You like to keep moving.

Organizing problems
You can't sit long enough to get your work done and you're easily distracted. You're too busy to tidy up between tasks.

Susan couldn't sit still for long. When she got up to get a snack, she forgot about her work and started chopping vegetables and preparing dip. She lost track of time, which caused her to feel stressed later when she was in a time crunch. She was losing sleep and feeling anxious.

Can you relate to Susan? Are you falling behind in your work, making it increasingly difficult for you to catch up? Are you frustrated with the lack of clear workspace every time you want to work on a project?

How can you satisfy your natural preference to keep moving yet still be able to complete your tasks?

Organizing solutions

Following are some tools and techniques you can use that fit your "let me do it" preference.

Remove the obstacles

Anything that keeps you confined is blocking you from processing your thoughts and absorbing information.

- Continue to take regular breaks every half hour but set a timer for five minutes at the beginning of each break and return to the task at hand when it beeps. Or alternate between two activities for a change of pace.
- Get physically active before sitting for extended periods of time. Run up and down the stairs or dance to one song before sitting down to work.
- Sit on an exercise ball instead of in a chair when seated at your computer. The physical movements required for you to keep your balance will help

you to process information more effectively. Another option is to use a swivel chair.

• Consider standing at a countertop to do your work rather than sitting. This works especially well for folding laundry, doing art projects, or any "assembly line" type of work.

• Make sure the temperature of the room you are working in is comfortable and that you're not wearing restrictive clothing. Cooler temperatures are usually preferable.

Stay focused

• Music in the background will keep you moving, and this in turn will help you to stay focused.

• Take notes, even if you're unlikely to refer back to them. Use point form and draw arrows and circles. Switch frequently from markers to pens to highlighters.

• Use pens with different colors of ink to represent different things. For example:
   ◦ Blue = general notes
   ◦ Red = important
   ◦ Green = follow up

• Use colored flags to mark the pages of a book or notes. You can even coordinate the colors with your note-taking pen colors.

• Try drawing your notes. Draw something that reminds you of what is being discussed and label your drawing with all of the appropriate information.

• Take a small stress ball to classes or meetings and squeeze it when you get the urge to move.

- Keep items on your desk that you can fidget with.
- Reposition your desk so you're sitting near a window or door.
- Make sure you have plenty of legroom so you're not always bumping into things.
- Designate a shelving unit with bins or baskets for each project in progress.
- Use breathing and relaxation techniques to help you to stay focused while working on important tasks.

Make motion your best friend

- When shopping for storage items, choose products on wheels, such as rolling filing carts, under-the-bed organizers that slide, and so on.

Rolling file cart

- When trying to process information, walk back and forth with your notes or use index cards. Limit the amount of information on each card.

Under-the-bed organizer

- Sit in a rocking chair when reading.

Make filing an action-oriented activity

If you are a kinesthetic learner, you will likely be looking for an excuse to move. Keep items just slightly out of reach.

- Use wall files for current projects and daily files. Install them high enough to require you to stand up to reach them.
  - Position your filing cabinet a few steps away from your desk so you have to get up several times or roll your chair to reach it.
  - If you prefer a literature sorter to a filing cabinet, place it on a table or credenza within rolling distance of your desk, but not within arm's reach when you're seated. Literature sorters usually have three vertical and at least eight horizontal compartments to store your documents. They are constructed of economical, lightweight corrugated paper, melamine, laminated wood, fiberboard, or high-impact plastic.

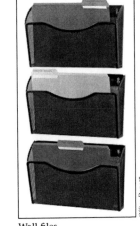

Wall files

  - Instead of traditional notebooks, use binders with sheet protectors. Use stickers to make key information stand out.

Literature sorter

Filers vs. pilers

If you're a piler, you may prefer to use a literature sorter (see page 52) or letter trays to organize your paperwork. Or try putting a desktop organizer tray on your desk to keep that pile manageable and papers easy to retrieve. This is a fit with your natural habit of stacking papers flat.

If you're a filer, you may prefer a vertical filing system like a rolling cart (see page 51), a crate, or a desktop file box. Be sure you position them no closer than swivel distance from your desk.

Desktop organizer tray   Desktop file box

Choose storage items with texture

- Use containers that appeal to your sense of touch, such as wicker baskets or canvas cubes.
- Choose organizing supplies that are pleasing to the touch, such as leather-covered planners, pens with cushioned grips, and so on.

Mind your time

- Use an electronic calendar to keep track of your appointments.
- Plan your activities but allow for flexibility in your schedule so you have the freedom to change plans when you need to.

- Make note of appointments, due dates, birthdays, and other special occasions and schedule time for regular tasks such as paying bills.
- Keep your schedule where you will see it often.
- To increase your productivity, schedule important or difficult tasks that require focus and concentration for the time of day when you're most alert and energetic. If you're a morning person, get up a little earlier and do them first thing. If you're a night person, schedule them for later in the day. The job will take longer if you're working on it during your non-peak hours. Tackle easier chores or enjoy leisure activities during your downtime.
- If you find yourself procrastinating over a task you don't like to do, schedule a favorite activity for right after it. You'll get the dreaded task done more quickly if you're looking forward to moving on to the preferred activity.
- Plan your day every morning (or the night before, if you prefer), using a personal calendar or planner. Place a sticky note on the front and list on it the things you must do that day. Cross items off the list as you complete them.
- Other options for keeping track of your weekly schedule include:
  - A bulletin board with the days

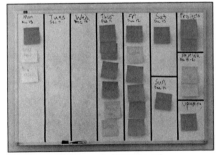

Weekly schedule on a bulletin board

of the week across the top and index cards or sticky notes with a task written on each one placed under the days. Remove each card or sticky note when the task on it is completed.

○ A whiteboard with days of the week across the top and tasks written under the days. Hang it across the room and check off or wipe off each task as it is completed.

○ Use technology: Download applications to your PDA or phone that will keep track of both appointments and to-do lists. Find ones that will back up to ensure that no items are lost. Set reminders by using alarms on the to-do items themselves or by setting an alarm that goes off at the same time every day. Use this time to plan your day and go through your list. You may also want to set an alarm for an hour before you leave work. This is a great time to review your list and make sure you have accomplished everything you set out to do that day, as well as to add follow-up items for the next day.

○ Use your refrigerator as a magnet board.
  – Divide the front of the fridge into three zones: Today, This Week, and Upcoming.
  – Each morning, move magnets,

Refrigerator to-do's

fliers, and notes to be done today into the Today zone. As new events and to-do's come in, place them in the appropriate zone.

– Each time you go past the refrigerator, update your zones by removing finished tasks. The goal is to have an empty Today zone each evening.

Staying Organized

Maintenance strategies for the kinesthetic learner

- Choose a calendar that works best for you and make it interactive. Use sticky notes and/or highlighters to mark important dates. Check off tasks once completed.

- Use sticky notes when blocking off time on your calendar for various tasks. This gives you the flexibility to move the task to another day and time if something else comes up that you prefer or need to do.

- Place all your hangers facing one direction in your closet. Every time you wear an item and return it to the closet, switch the direction of the hanger you place it on. At the end of the season, let go of clothing items on any hangers that have not been switched. This is a great reality check; it will reveal to you what you really do wear vs. what's just taking up space.

- Place all your kitchen gadgets and small appliances in a box. If you use an item from the box, assign it a proper home in your kitchen storage area. After three months, give away the items that are still in the box.

- Invest in a shredder and keep it in the corner of your home office to shred documents with any personal information on them. When you want to take a break from working on the computer, go through some old files and see what you can shred in fifteen minutes or less.

- Work in short bursts on a variety of projects but have an easily accessible place to store all the materials for each project separately. This could be a shelving unit with labeled bins, baskets, or portable file boxes (one for each project). If space is limited, use one binder for each project and store them on shelves. Use sheet protectors in the binders to save time and steps when placing papers inside.

- Choose one day each week and set a timer for fifteen minutes to walk around with two bags, one for trash and one for giveaway items. Walk around your home and challenge yourself to find five items to discard. These can be items in plain sight or in closets or drawers. Consider choosing a closet or one set of drawers to tackle each week.

- Never leave a room without looking around to see if you can take a few items with you that belong where you're going.

- Introduce just one or two new systems a month to avoid overload. Use your new systems consistently and modify them as you go along to best fit your needs. Resist giving up entirely on a system. Usually all it needs is some tweaking to fit you better (similar to how a new suit in your size may still need a few alterations).

- Reassess systems after any major life change, such as career, marriage, divorce, childbirth, and so on. Although your style will remain consistent, your needs will not remain the same forever. Schedule time to re-evaluate and modify your systems when necessary.

3

Organizing as an
Auditory Learner

Hearing Is Remembering

Y̶ou know you're an auditory learner if listening to a variety of music styles stimulates you and you wear earphones as a wardrobe accessory.

You enjoy spending time on the phone and prefer to hear directions rather than read them.

You find it easier to concentrate with the radio or television on in the background, yet you are easily distracted by external sounds like honking, ringing phones, or conversations in the hallway.

Do You Fit the Profile of an Auditory Learner?

You fit if you:

- Are distracted in noisy environments
- Notice background music
- Like to study by reading out loud
- Like to study in groups or with a friend

- Follow verbal directions best
- Learn best by listening
- Express ideas well verbally
- Tend to give detailed directions giving landmarks and not just street names
- Like collaborative work
- Remember names
- Remember facts and figures easily

Your interests may include:

- Listening to a variety of music
- Playing a musical instrument or singing
- Listening to audiobooks, podcasts, and talk radio
- Debating
- Public speaking
- Spending time with friends in locations where you can talk and be heard

Career interests for auditory learners may include:

- Salesperson
- Lawyer
- Politician
- Musician
- Motivational speaker
- Reporter
- Teacher
- Translator
- Poet
- Speech-language pathologist
- Doctor

Case Study: Meet Michelle

Is this your story, too?

Michelle is married and in her thirties. She works as a high-school music teacher.

When I met with her, she told me her biggest challenge was keeping track of all the messages she receives on her voice mail, both on her cellphone and home phone.

Although the school buzzer would alert her when each class was over at school, she often lost track of time at home and usually showed up late for appointments.

Michelle found it difficult to follow lists, so she was behind in her tasks.

She often got lost when she tried to follow written directions to her destination.

She confided that though she loves to learn, she finds it hard to focus when reading the books her colleagues recommended.

"I've tried doing my class prep work in the teachers' lounge but didn't get much accomplished because it was too noisy," she said.

Michelle told me she was happiest when listening to music or talking to friends on the phone. Although she was required to take courses for personal development, she didn't like studying for exams alone. She preferred to get together with a classmate and take turns asking questions.

Why did Michelle want to get organized?

"I need to keep on top of things so I can feel in control," she said. "I hate always racing to keep

up and feeling as if things are slipping through
my fingers."

Assessing the space

When I took a closer look at her space, the first thing
I noticed was her extensive CD collection, which was
organized by genre. Michelle also had a state-of-the-
art stereo system in the dining room and a surround
sound system hooked up to the TV in the family
room.

Finding the fit

Although I had quickly spotted many clues in
Michelle's surroundings to her learning style, I asked
her a few more questions to confirm my assessment.

What was she like in a learning environment?

Michelle told me that when she attends meetings
or workshops, she likes the door to be closed so she
can hear the speaker without outside interruptions.

"I also like to sit near the front so I can hear
clearly," she said, adding that, when permitted,
she tapes classes so she can listen to them later.

"What are you like when learning a new skill?"
I asked.

"I prefer to have someone talk me through the
steps."

I determined that Michelle was an auditory
learner.

Ready, Set, Go

Motivating the auditory learner to get started

Beginning the decluttering process is usually the hardest part. Putting it off makes the task all the more daunting.

Here are some tips on how to get the ball rolling if you are an auditory learner.

- Set your cellphone, your watch, or your computer to remind you to get started.
- Record your shopping list on your cellphone or small tape recorder as a reminder of what to purchase.
- Tune into your favorite radio station or put on some upbeat, danceable music that will keep you moving.
- Set a timer so you know when to end the organizing session.
- Consider inviting a friend over to converse with you during the process.

Organizing Strategies for the Auditory Learner

Organizing preference

You like to be told, not just shown.

Organizing problems

Written instructions are ineffective and difficult to remember.

You may be avoiding responding to e-mails because you prefer to make phone calls.

You may be afraid to file your papers because you might forget the name of the file on the label.

In the past, you may have been given lists of things to do but either couldn't find them when you needed them or forgot you had them in the first place.

You have difficulty focusing on a task when there are too many noisy distractions.

This is what happened to Michelle. She felt both overwhelmed and distracted by the sounds around her.

Can you relate to Michelle?

How can you satisfy your natural preference to hear things instead of seeing them yet still be able to find what you need?

Organizing solutions

You might try discussing your plan with others to help you fix it in your mind and to motivate you to make it a reality.

Following are some tools and techniques you can use that fit your preference for verbal cues.

Eliminate noisy distractions

- Listen to music through high-quality earphones to muffle outside noise. This will help you to focus on your work.
- Avoid sitting near a door or a window to prevent outdoor activity from interfering with your concentration. Close the office door when you're on a deadline; this will help you to eliminate external distractions and stay on task.

- If you can't reconfigure your office to eliminate external interruptions, consider working in another room (e.g., boardroom) when you're on a deadline and have to stay on task.
- Background music without words may be less distracting when you need to focus on important tasks. Invest in a set of white-noise headphones if you find auditory distractions are making it hard for you to stay on track.
- Close your e-mail program or disable the e-mail alert feature when working on urgent or important tasks that require your full attention.

Mind your messages

Since you prefer to communicate by phone rather than by e-mail, you need to set up a system to keep track of your calls.

- Keep a notebook by your phone to record any information left on your voice mail and for taking notes during your calls.
- When making calls, keep phone logs to remind you of the people you called and the purpose of the call. List any actions you agreed to take or any follow-up that's required.
- Leave reminder messages for yourself on your own voice mail.
- If you receive an e-mail that requires a long response, consider calling the person instead.
- Give people your phone number and tell them it is the fastest way to reach you; this will reduce the number of e-mails you receive.

Record it to remember it

When it comes to retaining information for future use, it's best to record it in a way that makes it easy to play back.

- Use your cellphone or a small tape recorder to record each day's tasks and appointments.
- Use a recording device like the Livescribe™ Pulse™ Smartpen. This pen simultaneously records and links everything you write to an audio recording that can be uploaded onto your computer, where it can be searched and reviewed. (See the Further Resources section at the end of this book.)
- Record workshops you attend (ask permission) so you have the information when you want to refer back to it.
- Download tele-classes and audiobooks to your iPod or MP3 player, or put them on a CD, so you can listen and learn while traveling.
- Use background music to inspire you while doing paperwork.

Use sounds as reminders

Sounds will jog your memory and keep you on track.

- Set your watch to beep every hour so you don't lose track of time.
- Use a wall clock that makes a sound you like every hour to help you to keep track of the time passing.
- Use alarms or timers with beeps for starting or stopping your tasks or to alert you to an important appointment.
- Keep track of the passage of time with music.

For example, if you want to work on a task for fifteen minutes, play three five-minute songs.

- Have a standard thirty-minute mix to study or work to. By using the same music each time, your brain will filter it as background noise and keep you better focused on the task at hand. (Skip the shuffle feature because it will undermine the purpose of using the same mix.)

Talk yourself through projects

- When reading how-to books or instructions, read them aloud. Stop periodically and have a conversation with yourself about what you have just read.
- When others give you instructions, repeat them, or rephrase them in your own words.
- When organizing your space, talk yourself through each step as if you're explaining your actions to someone else. Tell yourself out loud where you're putting things as you're doing it and you will have more success finding them later.
- Don't be afraid to sub-vocalize when reading important or dense information. You will both understand and remember it longer. (Sub-vocalizing is reading to yourself by moving your lips without making audible sounds.)
- Choose music that inspires you for the activity at hand (danceable for work that requires movement, tranquil for tasks that require focus, favorite happy melodies for tasks that may feel long and tedious).

Talk to others

- If you want to recall things you've learned, get together with a friend or a group of friends and discuss them.
- When making decisions, have a friend ask you questions to make it easier for you to decide.

Set up a "logical" filing system

- Separate files by category and organize them alphabetically within the category.

Literature sorter

- Keep personal files separate from business files.
- Write short clues for yourself on the outside of file folders so you can quickly identify the types of information inside. For example, if you're keeping hand-outs from a meeting or class for future reference, make note of what it was in the handout that prompted you to keep it.

Desktop file box

Rolling file cart

Filers vs. pilers

If you're a piler, you may prefer to use a literature sorter or letter trays to organize your paperwork.

This is a fit with your natural habit of stacking papers flat. You may also want to try putting a desktop organizer tray on your desk to keep that pile manageable and papers easy to retrieve.

Desktop organizer tray

If you're a filer, you may prefer a vertical filing system like a rolling cart, filing cabinet, or desktop file box. Be sure you position files no farther than swivel distance from your desk.

Map it and speak it

- Instead of conventional note-taking for review purposes, use flow charts, outlines, and mind-maps, then read them aloud.

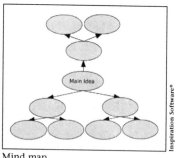

Main Idea

Mind map

- Create columns of space next to your notes and reserve that space for personal thoughts that come to mind while taking the notes.

Use technology as a tool

- Many computers have a built-in speech program that will read out any windows that pop up. You can set reminders to be read to you for immediate action and auditory reinforcement.

  ○ These same speech programs can also be set

to read any highlighted section when you input the shortcut keys. This is a great way to hear what you have just written – to help you to catch mistakes and refine your writing or just to listen to any text you have in a document, e-mail, or even from a Website.

o To locate these speech programs, check your computer's system preferences or help menu. (Such programs are usually under the keyword "speech.")

- Invest in a dictation program. You will find that you can plow through your work quickly once you have learned to use the program.
- Play the same music mix each time you are working on or studying for a subject. When you take the test, recall the song that was playing as you read the section with the answer to the question at hand. This can help you to recall the information.

Staying Organized

Maintenance strategies for the auditory learner

- Set your computer so it opens and reads your to-do list each time you start it up.
- Create specialized music mixes for different types of tasks and have them on hand to keep you focused and on track.
- Make a regular date for a friend or co-worker to come over and keep you company while you do your filing. Explain your reasoning to this person when choosing which file to place the various documents in. Talking this out not only will

enable you make better decisions about where to
file the papers, it will also help you to remember
where you filed them.

- Turn off your e-mail alert and phone for a
  short time every day to work on priority tasks.
- Always take notes during your phone calls and
  jot down any information left on your voice mail
  in a notebook used only for this purpose. After
  reviewing your messages, pull out your to-do list
  and write down any action steps or follow-ups
  resulting from the calls.
- When you are placed on hold while at your
  desk, put the phone on speaker and clean out
  a file while you listen to the music at the other
  end. This is a great way to turn a nuisance into
  an opportunity to be productive.
- Designate a regular day each week to walk around
  your home and find five items to discard. Set a
  timer for fifteen minutes and put on some music
  or an audiobook to listen to while you work.
  Carry two bags with you: one for trash and one
  for giveaways.
- Avoid overload by introducing just one or two
  new systems a month. Use your new systems
  consistently and modify them as you go along
  to best fit your needs. Usually all a system needs
  is some tweaking to fit you better (similar to
  how a new suit in your size may still need a
  few alterations).
- Reassess systems after any major life change,
  such as career, marriage, divorce, childbirth, and
  so on. Although your style will remain consistent,

your needs will not remain the same forever, so schedule time to re-evaluate and modify your systems when necessary.

4

When Organizing
Styles Collide

W e're all wired differently, and more often than not we share space with people whose learning styles clash with our own.

Are you frustrated because the systems you put in place and agree on just don't seem to work?

Have you ever blamed others for their lack of follow-through and commitment?

The problem is more likely that your learning styles are colliding. If you want to decrease conflict and enhance your relationships, it's crucial for you to understand others and learn to work with their different learning styles.

Organizing Strategies When Dealing with Different Learning Styles

Organizing preferences

People living or working together will have their own organizing preferences. Too many compromises may create a system that crumbles under its own weight. Striking the correct balance takes some consideration and effort on everyone's part.

The process of creating a routine will be easier if you can work your way toward a common vision and understanding of how a redefined space and system will benefit each of you.

Create a plan that identifies what should be done without becoming preoccupied with what has been neglected in the past. Assign tasks and make requests in ways that make sense to the person responsible for doing the task – i.e., based on *their* learning style, not necessarily yours.

Organizing problems

Written lists may not be accessible to all or be read by all. Verbal reminders may fall on deaf ears. Things may be started but not finished.

Individuals may become frustrated as they become overwhelmed by the project or responsibility. They may simply shut down and procrastinate rather than ask for assistance.

Organizing solutions

The solution does not have to be complicated. Each person should agree to clear action steps and responsibilities that will keep things moving forward and create a routine that builds relationships.

Create individual systems first

- Each person should start by finding solutions for their own learning style by reading the chapter of this book that applies to them.

- Once they know what works best for them, they will be more likely to succeed in working with you to create and implement a joint plan.
- Create a list of the strategies that you plan to try implementing for yourself.

Be careful not to overwhelm people

Some people are motivated by a list of everything that needs to be done. Others may feel over-whelmed. Ask the person what works best for them or show them the following choices and have them pick the ones that would likely work best for them.

Types of lists:

- A short list of projects. A project would be indicated as "paint the den."
- *Or* a detailed list of projects including the steps and supplies needed. For example, not just "paint the den" but "measure the den to find out how much paint is needed; pick up paint and tarp at the store (we have brushes in the garage); clear the space; cover the floor and furniture; paint the den; guests are coming to stay in that room on the tenth."
- *Or* no list at all – just one step at a time. For example, "Please measure the den, then come find me."

Types of time lines:

- A large block of time set aside to complete the whole project.
- *Or* time scheduled for a piece of the project followed by a schedule for the next piece.

Deal with procrastination

- Plan a reward for accomplishing your task or your portion of it. The reward should fit the job and not bring other clutter or tensions with it.
- If you need pressure to perform, extend an invitation in advance to someone to come and see your space once it's organized. This way you will have to get it done. Shoving things out of sight won't be an option because the person is going to expect to see exactly how you organized that closet or set of drawers.
- Break the project into manageable parts. Write each mini goal on a separate piece of paper or sticky note. Have only one note out at any given time. As each mini goal is accomplished, put the note aside (but still within view). Place one note on top of the other. As the notes begin to pile up, you will have a visual reminder of your progress. Putting the "to be done" notes away and focusing on the "achieved pile" as it grows will motivate you to keep moving ahead.

Organizing at

Home

5

When Organizing Styles
Collide at Home

You've made it this far into the book, which means you're ready to make a change. The question is whether the people you live with are as committed to change as you are. One person can do all the tidying up, but that can lead to resentment, especially if the space all too quickly slides back into clutter and chaos.

The best way to approach any change is to do so together. This chapter gives you the tools to dialogue, plan, implement, and maintain change in a shared living space. It all depends on building communication and working with everyone's learning styles.

Ready, Set, Go
Motivating people living together to get started

Here are some ways to bring the people you live with together to get the project started and ensure that everyone will do their part to get organized and stay organized.

- Come together to share ideas of what each individual wants to see in the new, uncluttered space. How does each person hope to be able to use the space? What current challenges do they face in keeping the space organized and clutter free?
- Encourage each person to determine their own powerful reason for getting organized and why it's important to them. How will it benefit their life?
- Make organizing less of a chore by introducing elements of fun. Have races or contests. Who can fill the largest bag of their *own* things to give away? Who can clear a section or put things away the fastest?
- Have each person make a list of the things in the room that they use. Next, invite each person to list the items that belong to them but may not fit in that room in the future.

How to Blend Styles

- Becoming familiar with the other learning styles will enable you to make requests in ways that make sense to the person responsible for doing the task. It's important to note that it's most effective if the individual making the request presents the information in the other person's learning style. This means you need to know their learning style and they should know yours.
  - Have the techie in your house do a search

for phone and PDA applications that will allow you to send/add items to each other's electronic to-do lists. These are inexpensive or free applications that allow only designated individuals to add items to a to-do list by typing the item into an online application that will then sync to the phone or computer and add the item and any message attached to it. Eliminating extra steps makes it easier to remember tasks. Just keep in mind that even though you've added it to the list today, the other person may not necessarily have time to accomplish it today.

- Work together to define the intended purpose or uses of the space, and then have the kinesthetic learner write it on a large sheet of paper and put it up in the room. Not only have you engaged this learner, but by discussing the plan you have met the needs of the auditory learner and by providing a list you have met the needs of the visual learner. By engaging all of the learning styles, you have helped each person to understand the purpose of the project.

- Have the kinesthetic learner prepare a box labeled with other possibly better locations or rooms in which to store things. As you sort and find something that belongs somewhere else, put it in the appropriate box. When you have finished sorting, invite each person to grab a box and be responsible for putting things away in the room indicated on the box's label.

Staying Organized

Maintenance strategies for people living together

- Give each person different maintenance responsibilities. When jobs overlap, one person has a tendency to take over. This can cause resentment to build up. Avoid this by having a detailed written list of specifically who does what.

- After jobs have been delegated, have each person commit to a maintenance schedule. By agreeing to do what fits their style and time commitments, each person is helped to succeed. It isn't necessary for everyone to pitch in at the same time.

- If your job is washing the dishes and you agree to do them in the evening, commit to following it through by that time. This reduces frustration when others see the stack of dirty dishes still in the sink the next morning. You may have planned to wash them when you got up the next day, but that's not what you originally committed to.

- You don't need to have a deadline day if you have set days for specific jobs. An "everything gets done by Friday" policy isn't necessary if the trash is taken out as it gets full and is ready the night before pick-up and the vacuuming happens each Monday and Thursday.

- If keeping personal belongings in shared places is a problem, assign each person a basket to keep in the common areas. Each person is responsible for sorting the contents of their basket. Decide together, ahead of time, how often the baskets must be cleared.

- Two weeks after the initial "big clean," set a time

to meet and talk about what's working and what still needs tweaking. This is the time to work any kinks out of the system.

- Schedule seasonal maintenance. As summer moves to fall, take a good look around and move out unnecessary items. Either relocate them to your storage area or give them away. Big spring cleanings are great and are much easier if seasonal cleanings have occurred.

6

When Organizing Styles

Collide with Children

You believe you could be more organized but feel that given all the different learning styles of your family, it's too overwhelming and time consuming to even try.

You've found that writing notes may work for the older children but never for the younger.

You spend your days reminding others about their activities but sometimes forget to do the things you had planned for yourself.

This chapter gives you the tools to dialogue, plan, implement, and maintain change at home by building communication and meeting everyone's learning style needs.

Ready, Set, Go

Motivating the family to get started

Living with family members, each with their own needs and learning styles, can be overwhelming.

There are too many people with too much stuff and too little space to fit everyone and everything in.

Following are some ways to bring the family together to get the project started and ensure that everybody does their part to get things organized and keep them that way.

- Call a family meeting. Ask each member to prepare a few ideas about what they would like to see in the new, uncluttered space. How do they hope to be able to use the various rooms? What are the challenges they face in keeping things organized and rooms clutter free?
- Plan a time when the entire family can be a part of the process and put it on the family calendar.
- Have each person make a list of the things they use in the various rooms. Next, invite each person to list the items that belong to them but may not fit in the various spaces in the future.
- Make it fun for everyone by having races or contests. Who can fill the largest bag of their *own* things to give away? Who can clear a section or put things away the fastest?
- Play music or sing as you work; let family members take turns choosing what they think everyone would like to listen to.
- If you have children under the age of five, arrange for someone to pick them up just after the organizing has begun. This way they're there to understand the process and help get the ball rolling but gone when the real work begins and they would cause a distraction. However, it is

important to include children when making decisions about their belongings. Let each child choose their favorites first and assure them that these will be put in a special place in their room/playroom. Talk to them about the benefits of purging toys and how their donations can bring joy to other children. Then help them put the toys they are willing to let go of in bags and remove them from the space together.

How to Blend Styles

Keep it simple. The systems and strategies that work for families with different ages and learning styles are the ones that are simple and easy to maintain. Anything that requires three or more steps causes frustration. Complex systems end up relying on a single person to facilitate them, and you want all hands on deck.

- By becoming familiar with other family members' learning styles, you will be able to make requests in a way that makes sense to the person responsible for doing the task. If each member is responsible for giving information in ways that fit the others' learning needs and preferences, the whole family will succeed.
- Give auditory learners information verbally when they're able to listen to you, not when they're running out the door late.
- Visual learners need lists. If you find they never start their tasks or very quickly get off track, try giving them one or two related tasks at a time.

Otherwise, they may feel overwhelmed and shut themselves down because they don't know where to start. When they finish those two tasks, go on to the next tasks. Small steps climb mountains.

- Together, define the intended purpose and uses of the various spaces in the home.
  - Then have the **kinesthetic learner** write these on separate sheets of paper and put them up in the space.
  - This means the **visual learner** has something to see and relate to while they work.
  - The **auditory learner**, meanwhile, can relate to the planning discussion and can read aloud from the list at regular intervals, reminding everyone where they are on the list.
  - Ask the **kinesthetic learner** or younger family members to mark off completed tasks so that everyone sees the progress.
  - By doing this you have engaged all of the learning styles and have helped each person to understand the purpose of the project.
- Read to the family or have them read the descriptions of each of the types of learners. As a family, identify and brainstorm for each member what style fits them best and what tasks fit them. Create a master list of the suggestions the family wants to implement and place it in a prominent place until the process is complete.
- Have the kinesthetic person in the family draw out a room plan/map. Together, label where the new zones for keeping and doing certain activities will be.

- Create an activity or reward for the family for completing the task. (For example, "When we have finished organizing and cleaning the den, we can host some of your friends in that cleared space.")
- Have the kinesthetic learner prepare a box for each room or location. As you sort and find something that belongs somewhere else, put it in the appropriate box. When you have finished sorting, invite each person to grab a box and be responsible for putting things away in the room indicated on the box's label. Group work helps to prevent people from disappearing when you really need them.
- Duties should not rely on someone else doing something first. (One person clears the table of paper *and* then sets it for dinner.)
- Clearly identify how a person will get new and reminder information. This should be presented according to the learning style of that individual, not the style of the person giving the information. For example, giving a visual learner a list of what to bring home from the grocery store is much more effective than calling out the items to them as they head out the door. Ask auditory learners to call from the grocery store. Reading the list to them while they are there may work better for them if they have taken written lists in the past and forgotten to use them while shopping.
- Set boundaries. For example, if a duty is not completed before dinner, the individual has opened the door to some friendly reminders.

Prior to the deadline, give family members the opportunity to set their own schedule without reminders. (This provides them with an opportunity to earn trust and independence.)

- Agree on a system before anyone goes shopping. This way purchases will reflect the entire family's needs.

- Individuals should select their own personal planners or calendars. If they don't want to go out and get them, suggest that they look for them online. (See the Further Resources section at the end of this book.)

- Set aside a dedicated space for leaving things for one another. Putting reminders and mail in their room may mean they're not noticed and responded to in a timely manner.

- Set aside a regular time to talk and review upcoming events and projects.

- Use your refrigerator as a magnet board.

  - Divide the front of the fridge into three zones: Today, This Week, and Upcoming.

  - Each morning, move magnets, fliers, and notes to be done today into the Today zone. As new events and to-do's come in, place them in the appropriate zone.

  - Each time you go past the refrigerator, update your zones by removing finished

Refrigerator to-do's

tasks. The goal is to have an empty Today zone each evening.

- Compliment each person on what and how they are contributing to the family's goal. Be positive and give encouragement. This will help to build and maintain trust, as well as improve results.
- Ask for input regarding how well you are communicating information in the other person's style; they may have good suggestions for what would work better for them. Learning to communicate information in ways that speak to other people's learning styles is a skill set that will prove helpful far beyond this activity.

Staying Organized

Maintenance strategies for the family

- Plan a reward for the completion of the project. This can include going to a favorite place, doing a favorite activity, or getting something new. The family should all know about this reward so it's an incentive for them to keep going and finish the project. You may also surprise the family with this type of reward for maintaining the space and the new routines.
- Family members should identify what they will contribute to the group effort on a consistent basis. Give family members maintenance responsibilities that do not overlap. Overlapping duties can lead to one person doing all the work or no one taking responsibility. Avoid this by having a detailed written list of who is responsible for doing what.

- Create systems of encouragement. Thank or compliment one another. Offer praise when someone takes on more than the responsibilities they originally accepted.

- Give unexpected rewards. For example, ice-cream sundaes for family members who have fulfilled their responsibilities without having to be constantly reminded. Studies show that people are far more likely to continue behaviors and actions if they get sporadic rewards than if they are rewarded every time. Rewards and positive feedback lose significance and meaning if they are overused. People must maintain a behavior over a long period of time for it to become lifelong change. By giving unexpected rewards, you are both helping these habits to become routine and giving more meaning to each reward.

III

Organizing at

Work

7

When Organizing Styles
Collide at Work

Being a part of a partnership or team or just
sharing a workspace can pose its own challenges.
Individuals bring their own needs and learning
styles to work with them and blending them can
be a challenge. However, when everyone collaborates
on overcoming these obstacles, the resulting energy
and synergy can prove productive and rewarding.

This chapter gives you tools to dialogue, plan,
implement, and maintain change in a shared workspace by building communication and meeting
everyone's learning-style needs.

Ready, Set, Go

Motivating the team to get started

Here are some ways to get co-workers started on
the project of getting organized. These will also
ensure that all of the members of the team will
do their part to keep the office organized.

- Call a meeting and ask each member to prepare a few ideas regarding what they want to see happen differently in terms of how the workplace is organized. What are the current challenges they face in keeping the office's workspaces organized?
- Have someone (preferably a visual learner) read the descriptions of different learning styles to the group. As a group, identify and brainstorm the style that each worker fits. Ask everyone to contribute suggestions for what might work for them. Create a master list of the suggestions for implementation and place it in a prominent place until the process is complete. The kinesthetic learner may want to make and post the list. The discussion will appeal to the auditory learners.
- Plan to put aside a time when those involved can be a part of the process without other commitments or responsibilities. When the scheduled day and time arrives, make every effort to turn phones and computers off. If you must monitor messages during the day, plan to check them during predetermined breaks.
- If the office has a set method of filing, get a copy of the system instructions for everyone. If it doesn't have a method, use your planning meeting to create one. Having everyone label and file according to the same system will save everyone time.

How to Blend Styles

Becoming familiar with your co-workers' learning styles will help you to make requests in ways that make sense to the person responsible for the task.

It's important for the individual making the request to consistently present the information in the other person's learning style. This will make the request more effective. Of course this means everyone needs to know their own and everyone else's style.

- Participants should identify what they want and what they need.
  - Wants are negotiable and can be adapted to fit the group.
  - Needs are the areas that must be met for successful implementation and maintenance.
- Ask only for what you need and agree on how that information will be given to you based on your style. Then identify how you will present information in a way that will complement your co-workers' needs.
- Agree on a system before anyone goes shopping for office supplies. This way the purchases will reflect the entire team's needs.
- Individuals should select their own personal planners/calendars. If they don't want to go out and get them, suggest that they look for them online. (See the Further Resources section at the end of this book.)
- Set aside a dedicated space where things will be left for the others. Putting notes and mail on co-workers' desks may mean they go unnoticed and are not responded to in a timely manner.
- Set aside a regular time to talk and review upcoming events and projects. Compliment each other on what is working.

- Ask for input regarding how you are doing in communicating information in the other people's styles. Others may have good suggestions. Learning to communicate information in ways that speak to other people's learning styles is a skill set that will prove helpful far beyond this activity.

Staying Organized

Maintenance strategies for the workplace

- Participants should identify what they will contribute to the group effort on a regular basis. Each person should have different responsibilities that do not overlap. Overlapping duties can lead to one person taking over or no one taking responsibility for the activity.
- Schedule a quick monthly maintenance sweep. On this day each person is to organize their own area as well as any common areas they have been assigned.
- Schedule a day twice a year for everyone to review, cull, and organize files.

Conclusion

Are you ready to conquer clutter and transform your life, your way?

Imagine walking into your home and being surrounded only by the treasures you love and the items you use. Gone is the clutter that suffocated and shamed you. Instead of dreading the thought of walking through the front door, you look forward to the vibrant energy and tranquility that you know will envelop you.

Imagine walking into your office and knowing that papers have been dealt with and filed where you can find them quickly and easily. Gone is the clutter that stressed and overwhelmed you. Instead of having to tackle one crisis after another, you're clear on what your priority tasks are for the day and you're confident that you'll have enough time to complete them.

Imagine spending time with your family and

co-workers without blame, resentment, and arguments about tasks that are not getting done or messes that are not being cleaned up. You work together as a team and jobs get done almost effortlessly because everyone is learning and organizing in their own style. You unite with others in a shared purpose to shift from chaos and discord to balance and cooperation. Instead of feeling dread over getting and staying organized, these tasks actually become fun ways to connect with one another.

You can make it happen!

You now know your learning style and understand how to work with it, not against it. You have the tools and techniques to redesign your surroundings to support you and move you in the direction you want to go.

Now it's time to put the ideas in this book to work for you. At first it may take some time and effort to put the systems in place. But you will be doing so in ways that fit your organizing and learning style, not through the conventional ways you've tried in the past with little success.

This time, it's going to stick. Eventually you won't have to rely on discipline to get organized; you will do it willingly – even joyfully!

Start small – don't try to do it all at once. Choose one or two strategies from the book that fit your style and put them into place, then reward yourself. Once you've got those down pat, try a couple more. Gradually, one step at a time, you will organize every area of your home, your office, and your life. As you notice how smoothly things flow at home and at work, you will release the guilt and develop self-confidence.

You will also shift the energy around you and as a result your life itself will shift in unimaginable ways. This is when the magic starts. Positive things will begin to happen to you. Unexpected opportunities will open up. You'll sleep better and feel more energetic and focused. Your creativity will flow effortlessly. Your current relationships will become more harmonious. And you will attract new friendships.

Not only will your life change dramatically, but those you live and work with will benefit also.

We have worked with countless clients who have successfully used the tools and techniques in this book to embrace their natural style and bring order and balance into their lives. We encourage you to take the steps outlined so you, too, can reap the benefits of being organized in every area of your life.

If you find you need some support to kick-start the process or stay on track, give yourself permission to get it. You don't have to do it alone. Please refer to the resources section at the end of this book to find the support you need. In addition, you can visit our Website at organizingoutsidethebox.com for more information.

We hope you will write to us and share your experiences so we can celebrate your success together.

Further Resources

ONLINE

Here are some professional organizing associations that can help you to find a professional organizer in your area to assist you:

National Association of Professional Organizers:
  napo.net

National Study Group on Chronic Disorganization:
  nsgcd.org

Professional Organizers in Canada:
  organizersincanada.com

To find a coach in your area to support you, visit:

International Coach Federation:
  coachfederation.org

Online calendar:
  google.com/calendar

OUTLETS FOR ITEMS
YOU NO LONGER WANT

To sell items:
  kijiji.com
  craigslist.com
  ebay.com

To give away items:
  freecycle.org

To donate items:
  charityvillage.com (Canada)
  Goodwill Industries
    goodwill.org
  Habitat for Humanity
    habitatforhumanity.org
  Dress for Success
    dressforsuccess.org

ORGANIZING RETAILERS

Home

Bed, Bath and Beyond
  Canada: **bedbathandbeyond.ca**
  U.S.: **bedbathandbeyond.com**
    1-800-462-3966

Container Store (U.S.; stores will ship to Canada)
  containerstore.com
  1-888-CONTAIN

Crate and Barrel
Canada: crateandbarrel.ca
1-888-657-4108
U.S.: crateandbarrel.com
1-800-967-6696

Home Depot   homedepot.com
1-800-430-3376

Ikea   ikea.com

Lowe's
Canada: lowes.ca
1-800-445-6937
U.S.: lowes.com

Pottery Barn
Canada: potterybarn.ca
U.S.: potterybarn.com
1-888-779-5176

Target
U.S.: target.com
1-800-440-0680

Office/Home Office

Ikea: ikea.com

Office Depot
Canada: officedepot.ca
1-800-GODEPOT
U.S.: officedepot.com
1-800-GODEPOT

OfficeMax
   U.S.:   officemax.com
                  1-800-283-7674

Staples
   Canada: staples.ca
                  1-877-360-8500
   U.S.:   staples.com
                  1-800-378-2753

PRODUCTS

Livescribe™ Pulse™ Smartpen:
   livescribe.com

UPDATES

To sign up for updates, event notifications, and
newsletters (these sites do not share or sell information), visit:
   organizingoutsidethebox.com
   weorganizeu.com
   saribrandes.com

About the Authors

Hellen Buttigieg, CPO®

As an award-winning Certified Professional Organizer and life coach, Hellen Buttigieg has been providing clutter therapy to the organizationally challenged since she started her company We Organize U in 2001. As a popular TV host of a decluttering makeover show, she won the hearts of fans worldwide with her ability not only to cut the clutter but also to understand the reason behind it.

Hellen is a sought-after guest expert on both television and radio. She is a magazine columnist and has been featured in numerous newspaper and magazine articles across North America.

She is a member of the National Association of Professional Organizers (NAPO), the National Study Group on Chronic Disorganization (NSGCD), and Professional Organizers in Canada (POC). She has served on the board of POC.

Hellen is a recipient of the prestigious Harold Taylor Award in recognition of her outstanding contribution to the organizing profession. She is a dynamic international speaker who leaves her audiences excited about clearing the clutter and transforming their lives.

Hellen is available for personal coaching/ consulting and provides workshops on organizing and time management. You can learn about her programs and services by visiting hellenbuttigieg.com

Tanya Sorkin

Sari Brandes, M.Ed.

A leading speaker, coach, and educational consultant, Sari Brandes runs a successful international business that trains individuals, families, teachers, and organizations to access skills for success.

Sari has created and developed strategies that earned her degrees from the University of California at Berkeley and Harvard University's Graduate School of Education. Her learning philosophy and strategies, based on individual learning styles, empower individuals to identify and harness their strengths and overcome their weaknesses.

Sari's vision for each client is to help them implement a personalized strategy with techniques to achieve success. She is a member of several organizations, including the International Coaching Federation (ICF). Sari has been a popular presenter and motivational speaker at many conferences, including the National Association of Professional Organizers (NAPO).

Sari is available for personal coaching, speaking engagements, and customized workshops and training programs for groups and organizations. You can learn more by visiting saribrandes.com

Staying Connected

Do you have an organizing success story to share with the authors? Your story could inspire others. Send us your stories for possible publication on our Website:

organizingoutsidethebox.com

Would your publication benefit from an article about organizing?

Is your association or corporation looking for a dynamic and motivating keynote speaker or seminar leader?

Is your company interested in purchasing this book in bulk at discounted rates?

If so, please contact the authors at:

organizingoutsidethebox.com

LaVergne, TN USA
17 January 2010
170275LV00001B/44/P